Songs
of a
Christmas
Night

B. J. Hoff

Christmas is . . .

The majesty of God

in the humility of a child . . .

Glory in a manger bed,

Hope in an infant's sigh.

Today in the town of David a Savior has been born to you; he is Christ the Lord. This will be a sign to you: You will find a baby wrapped in cloths and lying in a manger. *LUKE 2:11-12*

May this be the Christmas when the world greets him,
not as a stranger to be swaddled in a manger,
but as the sovereign King of everything,
the Prince of Peace.

May this be the Christmas when all the world
becomes a Bethlehem, with every heart an open inn
where Christ, Emmanuel, may always dwell
as Lord of Lords.

He came to that which was his own, but his own did not receive
him. Yet to all who received him, to those who believed in his name,
he gave the right to become children of God. *JOHN 1:11-12*

Against the shadows of a winter's sky,

A star shone, bright and new. . . .

Among the shadows of the world today,

His love comes shining through.

The star they had seen in the east went ahead of them until it stopped over the place where the child was. *MATTHEW 2:9*

GOD'S YES

How many are the promises
That God has given us,
How great the confidence
With which we're blessed,
That we are his beloved,
Cherished children of his heart,
Inheritors of all our Father's best.

He has pledged to us a love
We can't begin to comprehend,
A love fulfilled and sealed by sacrifice;
He sent his only Son
As confirmation of that love—
God's every promise finds its *Yes* in Christ.

For no matter how many promises
God has made,
they are "Yes" in Christ.

2 CORINTHIANS 1:20

Peace must be more than a word
embossed upon our Christmas cards,
echoed in the season's carols,
or painted on a storefront.
It can be found only in a Person,
experienced only in a Presence. . . .
For Christ, and Christ alone, is our Peace.

For he himself is our peace. *EPHESIANS 2:14*

His birth is not a memory,

but a promise. . . .

His coming brought the dawn of hope

to every human heart. . . .

The rising sun will come to us from heaven to shine on those living
in darkness. *LUKE 1:78-79*

No heart too humble for his throne,
  No home too poor or lowly . . .
The presence of the Prince of Peace
  Makes every dwelling holy.

I will put my dwelling place among you. . . . I will walk among you
and be your God, and you will be my people. *LEVITICUS 26:11-12*

One night in Bethlehem, beneath a singing sky,
A royal Prince gave up his throne,
A Shepherd came to seek his own,
The Savior of the world was born
One night in Bethlehem.

But you, Bethlehem, in the land of Judah, are by no means least among the rulers of Judah; for out of you will come a ruler who will be the shepherd of my people Israel. *MATTHEW 2:6*

Cherish the wonder, the peace,
of a gentle Christmas. . . .
Let the holy hush of the Judean hills enfold your heart
and touch the season with abiding joy.
Remember Bethlehem,
welcome the Savior,
and share his love.

There were shepherds living out in the fields nearby, keeping watch
over their flocks at night. *LUKE 2:8*

The Lord is Our Shepherd. . . .

Let the children of his pasture dwell in peace.

He tends his flock like a shepherd: He gathers the lambs in his arms and carries them close to his heart. *ISAIAH 40:11*

The One who spoke creation's word
has come to us a stranger. . . .
The One who overcomes the world
lies sleeping in a manger.
The One who flung the stars in place
and set the sun above us
is the One who, in his matchless grace,
has sent his Son to love us.

When I consider your heavens, the work of your fingers, the moon
and the stars, which you have set in place, what is man that you are
mindful of him, the son of man that you care for him? *PSALM 8:3-4*

Lord, lift our eyes above the trimmings and the tinsel....

    Let us look past temporary things

        To see the lasting gifts which you have promised,

        The joy and peace that life in Jesus brings.

Every good and perfect gift is from above. *JAMES 1:17*

It Isn't Far to Bethlehem. . . .

Each time a heart receives the King,
God's love is born,
Hope's star shines forth,
New life begins,
And angels sing.

Everlasting joy will be theirs. *ISAIAH 61:7*

Prince of Peace
In swaddling clothes . . .

Son of God
In homespun robes . . .

Lord of Lords
In thorny crown . . .

King of Kings
Who came down
To seek and save his own.

He humbled himself and became obedient to death—even death on a cross! *PHILIPPIANS 2:8*

Look beyond the manger bed
and see the generations,
the multitude of nations
who have come this way before. . . .
History is gathered here,
the humble and the faithful.
God's people meet as one
as they approach the stable door.

That the body of Christ may be built up until we all reach unity in the
faith and in the knowledge of the Son of God. *EPHESIANS 4:12-13*

Once again he comes to knock

    at the heart of the world he created. . . .

        Time and again he comes to our hearts—

        the Creator in search of his own.

There was no room for them in the inn. *LUKE 2:7*

Our searching hearts still travel to the manger
    with hope that somehow spans the centuries. . . .
Once more we kneel before the tiny stranger
    and recognize the promised Prince of Peace.

So they hurried off and found Mary and Joseph, and the baby, who
was lying in the manger. *LUKE 2:16*

CELEBRATE THE GIFT

Celebrate the Light of Hope,
The promise God has given
To lift the human heart above
The things of earth to heaven.

Celebrate the Love of God
That broke through time to sever
The bondage of the human race
And set us free forever.

Celebrate the God of Peace,
Who sent his Son to save us,
Who bore our sin upon a Cross
And even then forgave us.

Celebrate the Gift of Jesus,
Light of every nation,
Loving Savior, Prince of Peace,
Our Hope and our Salvation.

For God so loved the world that he gave his one and only Son, that whoever believes in him shall not perish but have eternal life.
JOHN 3:16

Rejoice...

In the peace of this hushed and holy night . . .
In the wondrous glow of the Star's bright light . . .
In the Son who left home and throne above
To bring us the gift of his Father's love—

Jesus

We rejoice in the hope of the glory of God. *ROMANS 5:2*

His coming was quiet . . .

No clash of cymbals, no blast of trumpets—

Just the midnight song of angels and the awe-

filled sighs of shepherds

on a hillside hushed by holiness.

His coming is still quiet . . .

His call is tender, his pleading soft . . .

Just a whisper of love in the silence and a gentle

touch of promise

to the humble heart that bids him enter in.

I stand at the door and knock. If anyone hears my voice and opens the door, I will come in and eat with him, and he with me.
REVELATION 3:20

JESUS...

A name to subdue mighty oceans and nations,

A name to tame hurricane winds and wild beasts,

A name to call forth praise from all God's creation—

Yet so gentle a name that we call him our Peace.

Therefore God exalted him to the highest place and gave him the name that is above every name. *PHILIPPIANS 2:9*

Two thousand years have come and gone,

and still the Christmas star shines on—

Its light as bright, its hope as true,

Its glory old, yet ever new.

Jesus Christ is the same yesterday and today and forever.
HEBREWS 13:8

Who would have thought that he would come
so gently one dark night,
instead of riding on the stars,
adorned with heaven's light?
Who dreamed that he would trade a throne
for swaddling clothes and manger,
appearing to the world he made
as a helpless infant stranger?
Who would have thought this poor and humble babe
would one day be
the King we would adore and serve
for all eternity?

As the heavens are higher than the earth, so are my ways higher than your ways and my thoughts than your thoughts. *ISAIAH 55:9*

NAME ABOVE

He is Ancient and Ageless,

Beginning and End,

King and Creator, Redeemer, and Friend. . . .

ALL NAMES...

He is Lord of the Universe,

Almighty One,

The Promised Messiah, our Savior . . . God's Son.

You are to give him the name Jesus. *LUKE 1:31*